Ask Another Question

The Ten Plagues from a Haggadah illustrated by Otto Geismar and published in Germany in 1928

The Story & Meaning of Passover

Ask Another Question

by Miriam Chaikin

illustrated by Marvin Friedman

Clarion Books
TICKNOR & FIELDS: A HOUGHTON MIFFLIN COMPANY
NEW YORK

For Menachem Begin

Acknowledgment
With thanks to Rabbi Lynne Landsberg
for reading the book in manuscript form.

Clarion Books
Ticknor & Fields, a Houghton Mifflin Company
Text © 1985 by Miriam Chaikin
Illustrations © 1985 by Marvin Friedman

Library of Congress Cataloging in Publication Data
Chaikin, Miriam.
Ask another question.

Includes index.
Summary: Discusses the history and importance of
Passover, a celebration of freedom commemorating the
exodus of Moses and the Israelites from Egypt, where
they had long been slaves.
1. Passover—Juvenile literature.   [1. Passover.
2. Fasts and feasts—Judaism.   3. Jews—History—
To 1200 B.C.   4. Exodus, The]   I. Friedman, Marvin, ill.
II. Title.
BM695.P3C46   1985   296.4'37   84-12744
RNF ISBN 0-89919-281-5
PA ISBN 0-89919-423-0

HM 10 9 8 7 6 5 4 3 2

Contents

Introduction

The holiday of Passover celebrates the greatest theme in human existence — freedom. Some three thousand years ago, the Jews were slaves in Egypt. One spring night, as a full moon shone in the sky, they left that land. It was not an ordinary departure. They changed their destiny that night. For they marched away not only from a land but from a condition. They marched away from slavery, toward freedom.

The inspiring story of Moses leading the Israelites out of Egypt has fired the human imagination for centuries. The story exists in every language and in every corner of the world. Enslaved peoples everywhere have drawn hope from this episode in Jewish history. The Black slaves in America dreaming of their own emancipation, found comfort in the words of the spiritual:

> When Israel was in Egypt land,
> let my people go.

The Israelites left Egypt on the first Passover night.

> Oppressed so hard they could not stand,
> let my people go.
> Go down, Moses, way down in Egypt land,
> tell old pharaoh, Let my people go!

Passover falls in the Jewish month of Nisan (March–April), on the evening of the fourteenth day. The name *Passover* is newer than the customs of the holiday. In fact, some Passover customs are traditions from two other holidays, one more ancient than Passover itself.

Before the Israelites became slaves in Egypt, even before they arrived in that country, they celebrated a holiday called the Festival of the Paschal Offering. An offering was a sacrifice. There were no houses of worship then. Offering a year-old lamb or goat, burning it on flames, was the only form of prayer.

In the spring, lambs and goats give birth to their young. It was vital to the welfare of the ancient family that the new flock be born healthy. The cheese and milk that the family ate came from these animals. The

animals' skins were equally valuable. They were made
into clothing and tents. The paschal lamb was sacrificed at this spring festival as a way of asking God to let
the new flock grow up healthy. The exact meaning of
the word *paschal* is not known. All we know is that this
was the name given to the lamb that was sacrificed.
The holiday was often referred to as the Festival of the
Paschal Lamb.

Each spring, on the night of the full moon, a group of
related families celebrated the holiday together. They
built a fire in front of their tents and placed the lamb or
lambs over it. They smeared a few drops of the animal's blood on the door of the tent. This may have
been a mark to show that the family had made the expected sacrifice, the way people today put stickers on
their windows or on their car bumpers to show that
they have contributed to a charity or organization. Or
perhaps it was still another way of asking God's protection.

At midnight, when the lamb was roasted, the family

members divided it up and ate it. The Israelites were celebrating this holiday, Festival of the Paschal offering, on the night that they left Egypt.

The second holiday whose customs entered the Passover celebration is from a later period, a time long after the Israelites left Egypt. When the Israelites reached Canaan, present-day Israel, they became farmers. Now they depended on their crops as well as their animals for food. They celebrated the Festival of Unleavened Bread. Unleavened bread is *matzah* (plural, *matzot*). This is a wafer or any flat bread that has been baked with unleavened dough, or dough that has not risen. The Festival of the Unleavened Bread was also a spring festival. It took place at the start of the grain-cutting season. To give thanks for the crop and to pray for its welfare, people offered a grain sacrifice on the altar and ate only matzot for a week.

Because Passover touches so many points in Jewish history, it is known by several names:

> *Festival of Spring, Hag ha-Aviv* (or *Abib*)
> Festival of the Paschal Offering, *Hag ha-Pesach*

Festival of Unleavened Bread, *Hag ha-Matzot*
Season of our Freedom, *Zeman Herutenu*

The dramatic story of the departure of the Israelites from Egypt appears in the Bible, in the Book of Exodus. The Book of Exodus tells two stories. It is the account of the greatest event in Jewish history, the freedom from slavery that led to the birth of a nation. It is also the story of the beginning of the spread of God-based religion. Before the Exodus, only the Jews believed in one God. Egyptians believed in many gods. They worshiped their ruler, the pharaoh, and various animal gods as well. When they saw the wonders and miracles that the God of the Jews worked, they did not begin to worship God. But they understood for the first time that God was greater than all their gods. Even the pharaoh agreed that there was a power higher than himself.

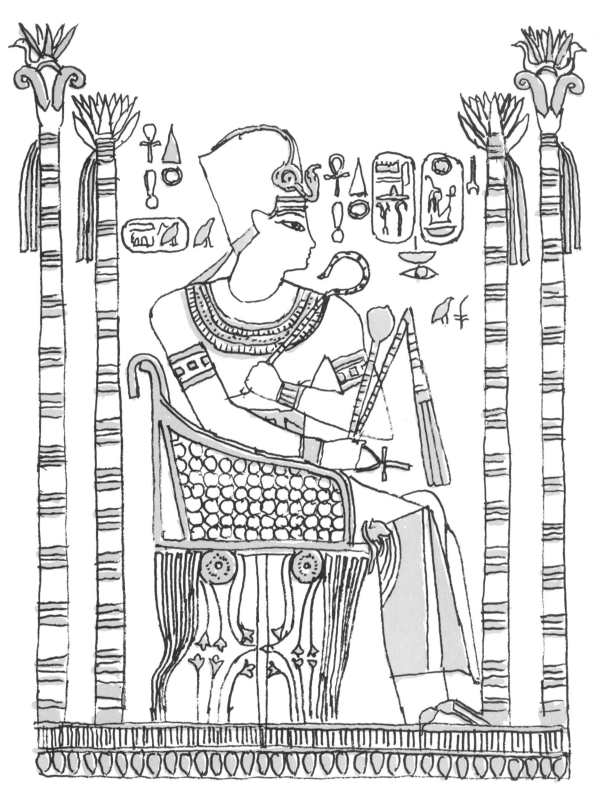

A pharaoh of ancient Egypt

Exodus

The events that led up to the Exodus from Egypt begin about four hundred years before the birth of Moses. They begin with Joseph of the many-colored coat, whose brothers sold him into slavery. His owners brought him to Egypt, where he became a great man. He was the trusted minister of the pharaoh, and the pharaoh put him in charge of Egypt's food supply. Egypt had the only assured food supply in that part of the world. The Nile, the longest river in the world, overflows during the rainy season, irrigating the earth and making it good for planting.

Egypt's neighbors were less fortunate. They often suffered from famine. When famine struck, they went to Egypt, where there was plenty of food. Famine in Canaan, is what brought some Jews of Joseph's time to Egypt. They came in search of food. And they settled in the town of Goshen, where they prospered.

The years passed, Joseph died, and new pharaohs came to the throne, one after the other. Then a pharaoh arose who objected to the presence of Jews in his land. Jews were different. They believed in one God and celebrated strange holidays. The pharaoh saw them as foreigners, even though they had been living in Egypt for years. He also thought that there were too many of them. The Bible tells us that he said to his court, *Behold, the people of Israel are too many and too mighty for us; let us deal wisely with them, lest they multiply.*

How did the pharaoh deal wisely with them? He made slaves of them. He had in doing this two purposes. Slaves provided him with the additional labor he needed to build pyramids and storehouses for his new cities, Pithom and Raamses. Bricks had to be made by mixing clay and straw together, and many hands were needed for the job. And besides, the pharaoh expected that the hard work would make the Jews too weak to have babies.

Half the plan worked. The Jews were set to work in the sun and given a quota of bricks to turn out each day. The work on the cities accelerated. But the pharaoh was disappointed to see that Jewish women continued to have babies. To add to his woes, he heard a distressing piece of news: the court astrologer had seen in a recent reading of the stars that a boy would be born among the Israelites who would set the slaves free.

To prevent that child from being born, the pharaoh ordered the two Egyptian midwives, Puah and Siphrah, to kill all boy babies when they were helping Jewish women give birth. The midwives did not obey the pha-

Jewish slaves made bricks for the pharaoh's new cities.

raoh. When the pharaoh questioned them, they made excuses. Impatient, the pharaoh took a more drastic step. He ordered all Egyptians to report the birth of Jewish boys so that these infants might be killed.

Despite his order, Moses was born. Moses' parents, Yochebed and Amram, already had two children. When Yochebed became pregnant, she hoped the new baby might be a girl. But the baby was a boy and therefore in danger. For a while, Yochebed succeeded in keeping the boy hidden at home. But then he began to crawl around. Soon he was bound to be discovered. Yochebed made a plan to save her son. The pharaoh's daughter was known to be fond of children, and she bathed in the Nile each morning.

Yochebed made a basket of reeds and coated it with clay and pitch to make it waterproof. One morning she set the baby in the basket and put the basket on the river. The baby's sister, Miriam, hid herself among the reeds so she could watch the flow of the basket. She saw the princess catch the basket and coo over the baby. Miriam had been waiting to see the princess's reaction. She ran forward and told the princess she knew of a nursing mother who could feed and care for the infant.

Everything went according to plan. The princess adopted the baby and named him Moses, which means "drawn-out-of-the-water." And she hired Yochebed to be the child's nurse.

Moses learned about the Jews from his mother. From the tutors at the palace, hired for him by the princess, he learned writing, arithmetic, astronomy, geography, and other subjects taught to Egyptian princes and noble sons.

One day, when Moses was grown, he saw an Egyptian beating a Jew. Enraged by the sight, he killed the Egyptian. Now he had to flee, for the pharaoh would surely take his life in exchange. Moses went to the land of Midian. There he married Zipporah, the priest's daughter, and lived as a shepherd.

As Moses was taking his sheep out to pasture one day, he saw a thorn bush in flames. That in itself was not startling. Dry bushes sometimes caught fire in the heat of the sun. But this bush burned without being consumed; it remained whole. Nor was that all. The voice of God spoke from the bush. God said that the

moses & zipporah

Moses and his wife were living peacefully in Midian when God called him to free the Jews of Egypt.

Jews of Egypt were in misery and crying for help. The Bible tells us that God went on to say: *I have seen the affliction of My people and heard their cries, and I have come down to deliver them from the Egyptians and to bring them to a good land, a land flowing with milk and honey.*

God told Moses to go to Egypt and free the Jews and take them back to Canaan, the land that God had promised to give them, where they could live in safety and dignity.

Moses hesitated. He was content with his new life. He had no wish to go back to Egypt. *Why me?* he asked, trying to get out of it. *The pharaoh is certain to kill me.* But for each excuse that Moses offered, God had an answer.

You will be safe in Egypt. This pharaoh has never heard of you.

How will I argue with the pharaoh?

I will put words into your head.

But I stammer and speak haltingly.

Take your brother Aaron and let him speak for you.

In a final effort to get out of going, Moses said the pharaoh would pay no attention to him. God assured Moses he would have whatever wonders and miracles he needed when the time came.

In the spring, on the day that the palace was open to the public, Moses and Aaron went to see the pharaoh. It was the season of the Festival of the Paschal Offering. And Moses' plan was to use the holiday as an ex-

The voice of God spoke to Moses from a burning thorn bush.

cuse for getting the Jews out of Egypt. Lambs were sacrificed for the occasion. Since Egyptians worshipped lambs, the pharaoh would think it reasonable for the Jews to remove themselves from Egyptian eyes in order to celebrate in the wilderness. There was an additional advantage to celebrating in the wilderness. It was possible, if the Jews received permission to leave, that they could just keep on going until they were safe in Canaan.

With Aaron speaking for him, Moses said to the pharaoh, *The Lord, the God of Israel, sends this message to you: Let My people go so that they might hold a feast in the wilderness for three days, in My name.*

The request met with scorn. *Who is the Lord?* the pharaoh scoffed. *What feast?* He said if the Israelites could attend three-day festivals, it could only mean they were idle and did not have enough to do. He doubled their burden. Up until now, the Jews had been given straw and clay for making bricks. Now the straw was withheld. They were told to gather their own straw and still turn out the same number of bricks each day.

Over a period of a year, Moses went ten times to plead with the pharaoh. Each time he greeted the pharaoh with the same words: *Thus says the Lord. Let My people go so that they might serve Me.* Again and again the pharaoh refused.

But each refusal brought another hardship on Egypt, for with the powers given him by God, Moses caused plagues to break out. The Israelites, isolated in Goshen, were spared. But the Egyptians were afflicted. The river was turned to blood, killing fish and making the drinking water foul. Frogs infested their lands, then gnats, then swarms of flies. Then a cattle disease killed their livestock. Boils broke out on their flesh. Then a hailstorm destroyed their crops. What the hailstorm missed was destroyed by an eighth plague — locusts. When the pharaoh refused for a ninth time to let the Israelites go, darkness lay over the land for three days.

The pharaoh's behavior was always the same. When a plague proved distressing, he asked Moses to end it, promising to let the Israelites go. But as soon as the plague was lifted, the pharaoh would change his mind.

The period of Jewish slavery ended almost as it began. Slavery started with the pharaoh who wanted to kill all newborn Jewish sons. It ended with the death of the firstborn Egyptian sons in the time of a later pharaoh.

The tenth plague was the last and worst of all. God said to Moses, *One more plague will I bring on the pharaoh and on Egypt, and then he will let you go; nay, he will drive you out of the land. For on this night I will send the Angel of Death through Egypt to strike down the firstborn males, and I will doom the gods of Egypt. A loud wail will rise up in the land such as has never been heard before and will never be heard again.*

One year after they arrived in Egypt, Moses and Aaron went to see the pharaoh for the tenth time. It was again the time of the Feast of the Paschal Lamb.

Moses repeated God's warning to the pharaoh. The pharaoh remained adamant as ever; again he refused to let the Israelites go.

Moses prepared the people for the events that were to come. He told them to celebrate the festival quietly in their own homes. *Slaughter your lambs and make yourselves ready for what the night might bring,* he said. He told them more. *Dip a leafy branch in the lamb's blood and smear it on your doorposts. Do not go out of your tents until morning, for the Angel of Death will pass through to smite the Egyptians, and when he sees the mark on the door he will pass over the door.*

The event that was to convert the festival into Passover was about to take place. The Israelites roasted their lambs and ate the meat with bitter herbs and unleavened bread. They watched the night from the doors of their tents, in awe of the work of the Lord. They began their meal but could not finish it. For a great wailing rose up in the land. The pharaoh's son, along with other firstborn sons, was dead.

The Egyptians had seen the power of God and grown afraid. Time and again they had asked the pharaoh to hearken to Moses' plea and let the Israelites go. Now they begged him to do so. In his grief, the pharaoh agreed. He sent for Moses and Aaron and said, *Leave! Go at once and worship your God, as you have asked. Take your flocks and herds and go, and ask a blessing for me also.*

The Israelites hurried to depart. They secured whatever valuables they possessed behind the sashes around their waists, and put on their sandals. The kneading troughs in which they had been making bread were put on their shoulders. Leaning on their walking sticks, they followed Moses out of Egypt. And they finished the festival meal they had begun earlier. As the Bible tells it, *And with the dough which they brought with them out of Egypt they baked matzah, for they had been rushed out of Egypt and could not linger.*

In the wilderness, the spirit of God went before the Jews, showing them the way. The Bible says, *The Lord went before them by day in a pillar of cloud, to lead them, and by night in a pillar of fire, to give them light.*

Moses had so far succeeded. But his troubles were far from over. The people quickly forgot the hardships of slavery and began to complain. They did not want to be in the wilderness. They did not like being thirsty. They wanted better, and more varied, food. They taunted Moses, saying, *We had bread and leeks and onions and other good things to eat in Egypt. And you bring us here, to kill us with hunger. Were there not enough graves in Egypt, that you had to take us to the wilderness to die?*

Nor was that all. Moses learned that the pharaoh had had second thoughts. It had been an act of foolishness to let the Israelites go. He had lost a big chunk of his labor force. The work on the cities had slowed to a crawl. *What is this we have done, that we have let Israel go from serving us?* he said. To correct the error, he sent his army out in chariots with instructions to bring the Jews back.

Moses appealed to God for help, and God gave him a miracle to perform. When Moses raised his arm over the Reed (not Red) Sea, the waters rolled back, and the Jews were able to cross over to the other side. But when the Egyptian army plunged with their horses into what seemed to be shallow water, the sea came rushing back, and they and their horses were drowned.

Grateful for their rescue, the Israelites rejoiced.

Moses sang, *God is my strength and my song, and my salvation. This is my God and I will glorify Him.* Miriam, his sister, took up her tambourine, and slapping it rhythmically, she sang, *Sing to the Lord, for He is highly exalted, the horse and his rider has He thrown into the sea.*

The Exodus story contains several Bible "firsts." The songs of Moses and of Miriam are the first songs of praise sung to God. The Egyptian pharaoh's efforts to kill Jewish male infants was the first plot to kill Jews. The pharaoh's plan does not succeed because of another Bible first — women rebels. The women who foiled the pharaoh's plot were the Egyptian midwives, Puah and Siphrah; Yochebed, Moses' mother; Miriam, his sister; and Bithyah, the pharaoh's daughter.

And now, safe at last, the Jews could move on toward Canaan, the Promised Land, the Land of Milk and Honey.

The Fruits of Freedom

The Jews, during this part of their history, experienced several "passovers." The Angel of Death passed over their houses. They themselves passed over the land of Egypt when they left, and then over the Reed Sea. They were no longer slaves. But they were not yet free. They remained in the desert wilderness with Moses for forty years. In that time, and under Moses' direction, they would pass over to real freedom.

Moses, the greatest figure in Jewish history, was known as the servant of God. Abraham and Sarah, the first Jews, taught their family to worship God alone. Moses taught a greater number of people that and more. He taught thousands of Jews in the wilderness the principles of civilization, principles that would make them a great nation. He taught them to live by the Ten Commandments, which became the basis of all their laws.

He taught them that the seventh day was a Sabbath, a

The Ten Commandments

day of rest for all. They were not to work on that day, neither were their beasts. The land, too, was to be given a rest every seven years, and no plow was to disturb it. Jews who could not support themselves became slaves in those days. Moses taught that slaves were to be given their freedom after seven years, together with some capital, to start a new life.

He oversaw the building of the Tabernacle, a tent set

aside for religious purposes, the first house of worship ever built to the one God.

He set up a system for judging complaints. As the Bible says, *And Moses chose able men from among all the people and made them heads, made them rulers of thousands, rulers of hundreds, rulers of fifties, and rulers of ten. And they judged the people at all seasons, the hard cases they brought to Moses.*

He taught the idea of justice, saying, *Judge the people with a righteous hand. Do not force a decision and do not consider the status of a person you are judging. Do not take a gift, because a gift clouds the eyes of the wise and perverts the thoughts of the righteous. Justice, justice shall you follow.*

He told them they had been strangers in Egypt and knew how painful such an experience could be. He told them that therefore they should treat strangers with kindness. Also, they were to take care of children, widows, slaves, and others who could not adequately care for themselves.

Refined and uplifted by these principles of civilization, the Jews passed over from being a group of twelve tribes to being one people, and from being slaves to being free.

They had yet one more passover experience in the wilderness. Before, God had always spoken to a single individual, such as to Abraham or Moses. In the wilderness, God spoke to all the people. And in that earth-shaking experience, the people swore to worship only God. Living in Egypt, they had adopted the practice of idol worship. Now they passed over from being idol worshipers to being a nation that worshiped God.

Moses had lived long enough to bring the Jews out of Egypt and to make a nation of them. But he did not live to accompany them into Canaan. Before he died, he imprinted the night of the Exodus on the minds of his people forever. He said, *Observe the month of Aviv [now called Nisan] and keep the passover to God, for in this month God brought you out of Egypt by night. On the fourteenth day of the month, at dusk, you shall kill a lamb without blemish. Sprinkle its blood on your doorposts and eat the roasted flesh in the night with unleavened bread and green herbs. Eat it in this way: tie the sash around your waist, wear your sandals, take your walking staff in hand; eat it in haste, for you left Egypt in haste. You and your children shall remember the Lord's passover for all time to come.*

How the Holiday Developed

In Canaan

When the Jews at last arrived in Canaan, Passover was the first holiday they celebrated. Joshua, Moses' disciple, now led them. He instructed them in Moses' teaching. Not much is known about how people celebrated so long ago. But it is likely that the people obeyed Moses' command to remember the fourteenth day of Nisan.

The Tabernacle, the portable shrine built in the wilderness, was located in Shiloh, in the north. This was the main shrine. Whoever could, went to Shiloh to celebrate. Others celebrated at their local shrines, taking their animals at dusk to the local priest, for him to perform the sacrifice ceremony.

There were two kinds of sacrifice. One was a holocaust, or total sacrifice. The entire animal was set on the flames and burned as a total offering. The other was a communal sacrifice. The organs only were sacrificed to God, while the animal was roasted on the flames and then eaten. A communal sacrifice was looked upon as a way of sharing a meal with God.

People roasted the lamb in a pit in front of their houses and sprinkled blood on their doorposts. They spoke of the miracle that had taken place on that very night, many years before. They felt under God's special protection on this night. And, as the lamb roasted, they watched the night with awe.

By midnight, the lamb was cooked. And all over Canaan, the Exodus scene was reenacted. People tied their belts, wore sandals, and held a staff, to recall the journey of their grandparents. And beneath a full moon, they ate roast lamb, unleavened bread, and a green vegetable from the new spring crop. They ate standing up, to give the appearance of haste.

In Temple Times

Several hundred years later Shiloh was no longer the religious center. Jerusalem had become the capital city. To replace the desert Tabernacle, King Solomon built a splendid new Temple in Jerusalem in 955 B.C.E. (Before the Common Era). It was said to be one of the most beautiful buildings in the world. So grand a temple called for greater pageantry. Musicians, singers, and choirs were introduced into the Passover celebration. And people from all over the land came to Jerusalem to offer their lambs and kids (baby goats) at the new altar of sacrifice.

We do not know exactly how they celebrated at that

time. Details begin to appear only centuries later. Documents and letters from the first century B.C.E. and the first century C.E. (Common Era) present a picture of the celebration. At that time, many Jews were living outside of the land, in other countries of the world. Pilgrims came to Jerusalem from everywhere for the celebration. The normal population of the city was 100,000. At Passover, more than twice that number of people crowded the city.

Early in the month of Nisan, shepherds prepared for the holiday. They selected their whitest and purest young lambs and kids, washed the animals in a creek near Jerusalem, and offered them up for sale. The animals were quickly bought up by local Jerusalemites and pilgrims. In almost every yard, tethered to a post, a spotless white lamb or kid could be seen.

On the afternoon of the fourteenth, trumpet blasts

sounded from the Temple. This was the call to sacrifice. It was followed by the cry of the priest: *People of the Lord, in the name of Him who rests in the great and holy house, Listen! The time for slaughtering the pesach lamb has arrived.*

At the signal, men brought their animals to the Temple gates. Priests, each in charge of a different function, were everywhere. Attendant priests kept order, sending in one group at a time. As one group entered with their animals through the gates, trumpet priests blew their horns.

People slaughtered their own animals. As they performed the act, musician priests sang songs of praise to God.

Besides the lamb or kid, the paschal offering, there was a second sacrifice. A holiday was a holy day. And so there was a separate sacrifice for the day itself. This was a *hagigah*, or holiday sacrifice. People brought grain or cakes of unleavened bread as a second sacrifice.

Then they hurried home, carrying the slaughtered animal in its skin, and put it to roast in an oven outside the house. Public officials distributed food to the poor, and soon the holiday was under way. Everyone put on white clothes. Women from foreign countries, such as Babylonia, wore the more colorful garments of their native lands.

Rich people ate seated on long chairs called divans, a custom borrowed from Rome, the great world power. They ate in a reclining position and drank wine with their meal. The meal consisted of a first course of lettuce dipped in salt water or vinegar, followed by the family's favorite dinner. Poor people stood or sat on benches and had no wine. They ate whatever they could afford.

Although the main festivity would take place later at the Temple, people first celebrated at home with the meal and a holiday discussion. Placed before the head of the house was a small table or tray with symbolic holiday foods: bitter herbs, matzah, a pudding of mashed fruit and nuts called *haroset*, and two cooked foods.

The leader explained the meanings of these foods as he told the story of the night of the Exodus from Egypt. The haroset, the pudding, stood for the clay the slaves used to make bricks. The matzah stood for the bread the slaves ate in haste the night they left Egypt. The two cooked foods were from the day's two sacrifices: a piece of lamb from the pesach offering and a matzah cake from the hagigah, or holiday, offering.

Everyone was in a merry mood; the children asked questions about the parts of the ceremony they did not understand. They may then have had a short nap. For at midnight everyone went to the Temple where, standing up, they ate roast lamb, matzah, and bitter herbs and sang songs of praise to God.

The Customs Are Spelled Out

As many years passed, the holiday celebration underwent changes according to the experiences of the Jewish people. Canaan became known as Judaea, then as Palestine. Jews lived not only there but in other lands. Some forgot how to celebrate Passover. They wanted to do the right thing but were not always sure what that was. Some people watched the night, expecting to see the hand of God that night. Some knew they were supposed to eat lamb with matzah and bitter herbs, but did not know in what order. The two together? One at a time? The Bible told them to cleanse their homes of leavened bread products for the holiday. What was the best way to do that? And how thorough did they have to be?

They directed their questions to the Sanhedrin, the Jewish religious court. The Sanhedrin met in Jerusalem until 70 C.E., and then in Yavneh and other cities. It consisted of seventy scholars and a president. The rabbi scholars studied the Bible closely, held debates, and made rulings. They said:

> • On Passover, all Jews should think of themselves as having personally escaped from slavery. For those who asked why, the answer was that they would still be slaves in Egypt if their ancestors had not been set free.
>
> • Everyone, not just the rich, should sit in a reclining position during the banquet.
>
> • Everyone, not just the rich, should drink four cups of wine (mixed with water) during the ceremony. Everyone was to contribute to a wine fund so that the poor might also have wine.
>
> • No one should be alone on Passover.
>
> • People should not watch the night expecting to see an act of God, because God is present at all times, not only at night. Instead, everyone should please God by doing a good deed. Open the door and call out into the street, *Let all who are hungry come and eat*.

Later the question about how to eat the matzah and bitter herbs was resolved by Hillel, a rabbi of the first century B.C.E. He created a custom by putting the *maror* — the bitter herbs — between two pieces of matzah.

Rabbi Gamaliel, his descendant, clarified things further. (Gamaliel was the teacher of the Apostle Paul.) Gamaliel said that three things at least must be present at the celebration:

1. The telling of the Passover, or Pesach, story.
2. Matzah, the poor bread, eaten by the Israelites when they were slaves in Egypt.
3. Maror, or bitter herbs, which the Israelites ate on the night that they left Egypt.

Later rabbis had other suggestions. They told people to make the celebration interesting so that children would not fall asleep during the long evening. *Make the night stand out,* they said. *Do things that would cause children to ask: Why is this done? Why that?* The idea behind all their rulings was in response to Moses' command to the Israelites to remember the Exodus night and teach it to their children.

So that people would know what was meant, the rabbis provided three sample questions for children to ask during the ceremony. Parents, relatives, or older brothers or sisters could give the answers they thought most fitting.

• Why is this night different from all other nights?

Asking the Four Questions

(Because on other nights we eat matzah and bread, but on this night we eat only matzah.)

• Why on all other nights do we eat roasted, stewed, or boiled meat, but on this night only roasted meat?

(Because our ancestors celebrated God's festival the night they left Egypt by eating the roasted meat of the paschal lamb.)

• Why on all other nights do we dip our food only once, and twice on this night?

(It is our custom to dip on other nights. We dip a second time tonight to remember that our ancestors dipped a leafy branch to smear lamb's blood on their doorposts.)

The Haggadah

The Passover ceremony is long and consists of many parts. There are prayers, stories, explanations, rituals, and songs. It was easy to forget something or to get mixed up about which part came first.

To help, the rabbis prepared a guide, a book telling people what to do and when and how to do it. The book contained the order of the ritual and also told the Exodus story. Since telling the story is the main part of the ceremony, the book came to be called a *Haggadah*, a Hebrew word which means "the telling." The Haggadah was already in use in 200 C.E. It may well be the first holiday "how-to" ever written.

New material has been added to the Haggadah over the centuries, making it sometimes hard to follow. Jewish history is long and eventful. And at each new crisis, the rabbis added another section to the Haggadah. Sometimes they dropped one. If two rabbis had differ-

הָא לַחְמָא עַנְיָא דִי אֲכָלוּ אַבְהָתָנָא
בְּאַרְעָא דְמִצְרַיִם כָּל דִּכְפִין יֵיתֵי
וְיֵכוֹל כָּל דִּצְרִיךְ יֵיתֵי וְיִפְסַח
הָשַׁתָּא הָכָא לְשָׁנָה הַבָּאָה

ent explanations, both explanations were included. An idea of how the Haggadah received its contents can be had from these examples.

New Sections Are Added

In the third century B.C.E., Egypt ruled Judaea. Egyptian soldiers could be seen everywhere in Jerusalem. This presented a problem on Passover night. The Exodus story, which had to be related, showed the pharaoh in a bad light. The Egyptians were certain to resent it. The Jews did not want to give offense.

The rabbis found a way around the problem. They added a new incident to the Haggadah, one that showed the pharaoh in a better light.

The incident concerned Jacob, a Jew, and his uncle Laban, an Aramaean (Syrian).

Jacob is the father of the Jewish people. His wives were Rachel and Leah. From them, all Jews are descended. The twelve sons of Jacob and his wives were the fathers of the twelve families that became the twelve tribes of Israel.

Laban tried to kill Jacob after a quarrel. (They later made up.) If Laban had succeeded, the Jewish people would not have come into being. The pharaoh's plan would have had less drastic results. He tried to kill only Jewish male children. If he had succeeded, the

A page from the Sarajevo Haggadah

Jewish population would not have grown, but the nation would have existed.

This thought the rabbis added to the ceremony, to demonstrate that although the pharaoh's intentions had been bad, the results of Laban's intentions would have been worse.

Questions Are Changed

In the year 70 C.E., Rome destroyed the Temple and the city of Jerusalem and drove the Jews from the land. Gone was the Temple that had been the center of Jewish worship for a thousand years. And gone were all animal sacrifices, including the pesach lamb. A change in the Haggadah was in order. The question about why roast meat was eaten on Passover no longer applied. The rabbis dropped the question and replaced it with another one:

> Why on all other nights do we eat many herbs and on this night only bitter herbs?
> (To recall the bitter lives of our ancestors, who were slaves in Egypt.)

Another change was also called for.

Driven from Jerusalem, Jews settled in distant countries, where they found different customs. For one thing, people did not dip lettuce in salt water as a first course. The words of the dipping question also had to be changed. Instead of, "Why on all other nights do we dip our food only once, and on this night twice?," the question became:

Why do we not dip our food even once on other nights, and twice on this night?

(Possible answers: We dip the first time to recall the night the ancient Israelites dipped a leafy branch into lamb's blood to mark their doorposts. Or: We dip parsley [or lettuce] the first time to celebrate the crops of spring. Or: We dip bitter herbs into sweet haroset to show hope, for our ancestors could not have survived the bitterness of slavery without hope.)

A Fourth Question Is Added

Rome was no longer a world power, Europe began to grow in importance, and people no longer ate reclining on divans. They ate sitting up, in chairs. The rabbis introduced a fourth question for the children to ask on Passover night:

Why on all other nights do we sit up to eat, but recline on this night?

(Because free people reclined in ancient times, and our ancestors became free on this night.)

The Open-Door Ceremony

European history between the years 500 and 1450 C.E. was often characterized by ignorance and superstition. For Jews, it was a time of great peril. The atmosphere was such that they could no longer begin the Passover ceremony by opening the door and calling, *Let all who are hungry come and eat*.

In the cities of Europe hundreds of thousands of Christian soldiers assembled for the Crusades. They were going to march to Palestine. Palestine, the Holy Land, was then under the control of the Arabs, who had conquered it in 638 c.e. The object of the march was to take possession of the Holy Land for Christianity.

For some soldiers it was a holy undertaking. But there were also murderers, robbers and other criminals among them. And the march across Europe to Palestine was an opportunity for plunder and acquiring riches.

The Crusaders terrorized and slaughtered thousands of Jews in England, France, Germany, and Italy on their way to the Holy Land. They destroyed completely the Jewish community of Prague in Czechoslovakia. When they arrived in Palestine, they destroyed the Jewish population of Jerusalem.

Eight crusades took place over a 200-year period, beginning in 1096.

In Spain a different disaster affected the celebration of Passover. King Ferdinand and Queen Isabella in the 1470s passed a decree that only Christians could hold important jobs. At the time, many Jews held official positions. The idea behind the decree was to force Jews to convert to Christianity. Spanish mobs interpreted the decree as a signal to riot against the Jews.

Jews who were alarmed fled from the country. Others converted and became what the Spanish called "New Christians." Some who converted did so only in order to escape the wrath of the mob. They were Christians outwardly, going to church, but practiced the Jewish religion in secret. They were called *Marranos* which means "swine" in Spanish. Some Jews remained Jews and lived in great poverty.

In 1480, Queen Isabella and King Ferdinand set up an Inquisition in Spain. This was a religious court that judged whether converted Jews were true Christians. The Inquisition was a field day for evil. Everyone spied on everyone else. If guests arrived at the home of a New Christian on the evening that was Passover, they and the New Christian family were reported to the Inquisition as secret Jews. If someone had a grudge against a New Christian, he reported that person as a secret Jew.

Spanish mobs attacked and killed New Christians they suspected of being secret Jews. Then they, and the Spanish nobles who incited them against the Jews, helped themselves to the property and possessions of the victims.

Sixtus IV, the pope at that time, wrote that the attacks against the New Christians were done "not out of love for the [Christian] religion and not for the saving of souls, but rather out of desire for enrichment."

The Inquisition ended some 350 years later, in 1834. During that period of time, some 400,000 people suspected of being secret Jews were arrested, interrogated, tortured, and tried. About 35,000 were burned at the stake.

The burnings were a public event. People came to watch. A prominent member of the community was given the honor of starting the fire. This type of mass execution was called *auto-da-fé*, an "act of faith."

The king and queen brought their campaign against the Jews to a climax. In May 1492, they issued a decree. All Jews were to leave Spain four months later, on August 2. Christopher Columbus wrote in his diary that he had set out in the same month "in which their Majesties issued the edict that all Jews should be driven out of the kingdom and its territories." Six members of his crew were New Christians, former Jews. Jews had lived in Spain for more than a thousand years. In 1492 between 200,000 and 300,000 *Sephardim*, Spanish Jews, left Spain for Italy, Portugal, and lands in Europe and North Africa including Egypt, and Palestine.

In England and elsewhere in Europe other blights affected the Passover celebration. Malicious Gentiles circulated false stories at Passover. Their purpose was to enrage ignorant mobs and make them rise up against the Jews. There were many versions of the same story. One version said that Jews had a disease that could be cured by baptism, the only other way to get rid of the disease was to drink the blood of a Christian child.

At Passover, ignorant peasants spied on Jewish homes in the belief that Jews were drinking not Passover wine but the blood of a Christian child. Some troublemakers went so far as to supply evidence. They tossed a dead child onto a Jewish doorstep to "prove" the charge. Too often, Passover in Europe was an occasion for Christian mobs to massacre innocent Jews.

Over the ages some popes tried to put a stop to the vicious lie. They pointed out that Jews were forbidden by their religion even to touch a dead body. Nevertheless, the "blood libel," as these false charges are known, continued.

In places where Jews were free of massacres, they were not free of "blood libel" threats. At Passover, they faced a dilemma. Danger lurked outside, and it was not safe to begin the evening celebration by throwing open the door. Yet how could they close the door? To close the door would look like a lack of faith. And God had worked miracles for their ancestors on that very night.

Opening the door at the start of the ceremony and shouting a welcome into the street was abandoned. But the act was kept as a symbol of faith. The door was opened briefly later in the ceremony. Opening the door also had a practical side. People could glance outside and see if all was clear, or if some danger threatened.

To help ease the fear the Jews felt, the rabbis added a little speech for them to make when they opened the door. *Pour out your wrath*, it began, and went on to ask God to be angry with persons who were bent on doing evil.

Elijah's Cup

After the Middle Ages, the ceremony of the open door led to yet another one.

Jews hold fast to the belief that the Messiah will one day come. The Messiah is most often thought to be an individual, a descendant of King David. But the Messiah may also be an event. The coming of the Messiah is expected to improve life for everyone and make the world a place of peace, harmony, order, and perfection. The Messiah will not arrive suddenly, without warning. Elijah the Prophet will first appear, as a sign that the Messiah is coming.

How did Elijah become part of the Passover ceremony? It happened this way.

The early rabbis had decided that four glasses of wine should be drunk during the ceremony because there are four biblical references to the rescue of the slaves. Later rabbis suggested that there were five such references and that five glasses should be drunk. This led to a debate. The rabbis could not come to a decision.

As a compromise, they put an empty glass on the table, to represent a fifth round. They decided, since the prophet Elijah will solve all problems when he comes, to leave the final decision to him. Soon, they began to fill the empty glass with wine, hoping to lure Elijah, and thus hasten the arrival of the Messiah. The glass became known as Elijah's Cup. And when the door was opened, everyone around the table rose to welcome the invisible guest and sing the song "Eliahu ha-

LEFT:
An 18th-century Elijah's Cup from Russia
RIGHT:
An 18th-century German plate depicting the four types of children

Navi," Elijah the Prophet. Elijah's untouched wine is returned to the bottle — unless mischievous hands pour it into glasses around the table to make it appear as if the wine has been drunk.

Four Types of Children

The story of the departure from Egypt that was told during the Passover celebration seemed not to be getting across to all children. Some were interested, some were not, and some did not even bother to listen. The rabbis concluded that one version of the story was not enough. There were too many different types of children in the world. The rabbis divided children into four main types: wise, wicked, simple, and very young. The story was to be told differently to each type.

The wise child is curious and asks questions, and should be told the entire story. The wicked child makes fun of the ceremony and should be told that God worked miracles for the others, not for him. The simple child does not fully understand what is happening; to this child clear and direct explanations should be given.

The child who is too young to ask questions is told, simply, "We celebrate because of what God did for us when we left Egypt."

This idea appears in the Haggadah in the form of a conversation that is read aloud. As a result, all children around the table hear all explanations and decide for themselves to which group they belong.

Current History Is Added

Jewish history is very long. And the Haggadah highlights, in a phrase or two, key episodes from this history. With the passage of time, current events become history. And two events that took place in the twentieth century have now also been added to the Haggadah. One event is the Holocaust, the organized killing in World War II of six million defenseless civilian Jews. The event was a tragedy not only for its victims but for the civilized world as well. The victims were slaughtered in a way and on a scale never before seen in history. The slaughterers who devised the plan and carried it out were not street mobs but modern, civilized people.

World War II began in the late 1930s. Until then the three darkest periods in Jewish history were the destruction of Jerusalem in 70 C.E., the Crusades, and the Spanish Inquisition. Adolf Hitler of Germany added a fourth. His first aim in starting the war was to conquer Europe. His second was to remove Jews from the world. How did he go about this?

Nazis, Hitler's soldiers, seized Jews and sent them to

slave labor camps, where they made supplies for the German army. When the Jewish laborers became too exhausted to work, they were removed to death camps to be scientifically killed. Systematically, in cold blood, in gas chambers and ovens invented for the purpose, the Nazis and their collaborators slaughtered millions of innocent Jewish men, women, and children in the course of World War II. One-third of the world Jewish population disappeared.

New words were needed to speak of the horrors of those times. A greek word, *holocaust*, which means to destroy wholly by fire, became part of the everyday English language. *Genocide*, which means the systematic killing of an entire people, was another new word.

Early in the war some Jews managed to escape the death chambers. Homeless and on the run, entire fami-

lies sought asylum in other lands. But for the most part, unlike their ancient ancestors, they could not pass over to safety.

Only Denmark, Sweden, and Shanghai, which was then under Japanese control, saved Jews by taking them in. Spain also accepted Jews. The Italian army and Italian civilians hid Jews and helped them survive. Individual Gentiles in Holland and elsewhere in Europe also extended a helping hand. But in the rest of the world, all doors were closed to the fleeing Jews. As a result, six million Jewish men, women, and children were killed in Hitler's death factories.

Passover during the war years in Poland was recorded by Emmanuel Ringelblum, a Polish-Jewish historian, who kept a diary. He, together with hundreds of thousands of other Jews, had been rounded up by the Nazis and forced to live in one area in Warsaw. They lived in cramped, unsanitary conditions in the ghetto, and under guard.

According to Ringelblum's diary, there was no food in the Warsaw ghetto for Passover 1941, but matzah was expected to arrive. A Jewish charity had arranged for a shipment. On April 11, the Jews lined up to receive matzah. But, along with the matzah, the dreaded ghetto guards also arrived. Guards had to turn over a daily quota of Jewish labor for the work camp. They plucked the number of men they needed from the line. For these men, the matzah line was a death sentence.

Grim and depressing though the times were, Ringelblum recorded an amusing incident. The ghetto was under curfew. Jews were not allowed in the streets after dark. Yet they wanted to visit friends and relatives on the holiday. A group of Jews went to ask permission to be in the streets after dark. When questioned, they explained the holiday. They received passes for themselves and also one for Elijah the Prophet.

Chaim A. Kaplan also kept a diary. He characterized the Passover of 1941 as a Passover of hunger, poverty, and spiritual darkness. The Germans had closed all synagogues. Kaplan's entry for the next Passover, April 1, 1942, says that skeletons, not human beings, walked the ghetto streets.

Early in the war, before the mass killings had begun, one group of Jews in the Bergen-Belsen concentration camp asked the camp commander for permission to celebrate Passover. The Jews were allowed to make matzah. Their table was a bunk bed, and a potato took the place of the six symbolic foods. The rabbi spoke about the night of the Exodus, and the children asked questions. To instill hope, the rabbi reminded those present that just as God had sent Moses to save the slaves of Egypt, someone would come to save them as well. His message worked. The people were in a better mood when they returned to their own barracks. Some told the rabbi the next day that they could hear the footsteps of Elijah accompanying them home.

By 1944, conditions had changed at Bergen-Belsen. There was no matzah, and no food. Jews faced starvation and death. They spoke this prayer at Passover:

> Our Father in Heaven, it is our desire to celebrate the Passover festival by eating matzot and avoiding leav-

ened foods. But our lives are in danger and our hearts are pained that we cannot observe your festival. Please save us soon and keep us alive so that we can observe Your festival and Your statutes with a perfect heart.

Some Polish Jews managed to escape to a part of Yugoslavia that was controlled by the Italian army. The Italians gave the Jews false identity papers, saying they were Italian Catholics. The Jewish children did not know they were Jews. It was too dangerous to tell them the truth. They might innocently speak of it and endanger the lives of their parents and others, for there were Germans in the area. On Passover night, at midnight, when the children were asleep, eight or nine couples celebrated Passover in secret, in order to keep in touch with their faith.

In the Warsaw ghetto, the Passover of 1943 was historic. On April 18, Passover night, the German army arrived in tanks and surrounded the ghetto walls. They had come to kill the Jews. Although the Jews had no chance against German tanks and bombs, they decided to fight back and die with dignity. Armed only with homemade hand grenades and pistols, Jewish men, women, and children fought the Nazis. The Battle of the Warsaw Ghetto, which began that night, lasted five weeks. Seven thousand Jews were killed. The fifty thousand who survived the battle were sent to the death camps.

The unspeakable episode of the Holocaust has been added to the Haggadah, as an event to be remembered and mourned over.

The second event of this century that was added to the Haggadah is a joyous one: the rebirth of the Jewish state after 2,000 years. Today, Jews in trouble have a homeland that will take them in.

The Haggadah responds to the times, and individuals sometimes add ideas of their own to it. The idea is usually one of "passing over" from one state to another. This may be a wish for a nation at war to pass over to peace, for a people in trouble to pass over to relief, for an ailing person to pass over to health.

Feminists might stress the role played by women in the Passover story so that these women pass over from being considered bit players to being seen as principal characters.

People also celebrate the natural world in adding to the Haggadah. They give thanks for passing over from winter darkness to the light of spring, for seeing the earth pass over from barrenness to the giving forth of blossoms and fruit.

The Haggadah will no doubt include yet other themes in the future.

How the Holiday Is Celebrated Today

There are three main branches of religious Judaism: Orthodox, Conservative, and Reform. Customs differ slightly in each branch. Orthodox and Conservative Jews celebrate the first two nights of Passover. Reform Jews celebrate only the first night, as do the Jews of Israel.

National customs also account for differences. Celebrations will vary between American and other Jews, for example. In general, however, all Jewish families will follow the pattern set down in the Haggadah. And all will seek to make the night interesting, especially for the children.

Most of the questions the children will ask arise from the one question: Why is this night different from all other nights? And most answers will be derived from the answer: Because our ancestors were slaves in Egypt, and on this night God set them free.

But before the Passover celebration actually begins, there is a ceremony the night before for children.

The Search for Leaven

The Bible says that people must rid their homes of leaven before Passover and that they may eat only unleavened bread, matzah, throughout the week. Ridding the house of leaven means removing all bread products and every bread crumb. To accomplish this, everyone in the family sets out together on a Search for Leaven.

The house has already been thoroughly swept and cleaned for the holiday. But, so that the search may show results, the mother places a few — usually ten — pieces of bread about the house. She also turns out some lights, to make the house dark and the search more dramatic. Then everybody sets out together with a candle or flashlight, a feather for sweeping up crumbs, a wooden spoon to catch the crumbs, and a paper bag to hold them.

When the search is over, the children put the paper bag with crumbs aside until morning. They have searched thoroughly. They are sure they have missed no crumbs. Still, just in case they have, to be safe, they make this little speech saying that they haven't seen any crumbs. *If there are any bread crumbs that I have not seen, let them be as nothing, as ownerless, as dust of the earth.*

The next morning, after breakfast and after the kitchen floor has been swept, they search again. Then they burn the spoon, feather, and paper bag in the backyard or the incinerator. And the children repeat once more the "I-never-saw-it" phrase in a somewhat different form. They say, *All bread that may be here, whether I have seen it or not, destroyed it or not, let it be as the dust of the earth.*

Helping clean the house of bread crumbs before Passover begins

The First Night of Passover

Jews come from two main cultures. Those who settled in the countries of eastern and central Europe are called *Ashkenazim*. They spoke the language of the land and also created Yiddish, a mixture of Hebrew and German. Those who settled in Spain when it was a Muslim country, and in other Muslim countries, are called *Sephardim*. They spoke Spanish and Arabic and also created *Ladino*, a mixture of Spanish and Hebrew.

Each group has a different name for the first night of Passover. The celebration consists of fourteen ceremonies performed in a certain order. Ashkenazim call the celebration *seder*, which means "order" in Hebrew. Sephardim call it *haggadah*, the "telling."

The Four Questions. The questions asked on Passover night need not be limited to four. Any number of questions may be asked. Answers may be matters of fact or of opinion. Questions may have more than one answer. The idea is to keep alive the memory of the night that the Israelites left Egypt, by telling stories and discussing that eventful episode. The four basic questions appear in every Haggadah. They appear earlier in this book, on pages 29 and 30, along with possible answers. For easy reference, the questions alone are repeated here.

- Why is this night different from all other nights?
- Why on other nights do we eat various herbs, and on this night only bitter herbs?
- Why on other nights do we not dip our food even once, and twice on this night?

• Why on other nights do we sit up to eat, and re-cline on this night?

The Lessening of Our Joy. Another ritual was added to the Haggadah in the sixteenth century. It involves wine, which is the symbol of joy. The ritual takes place at that point in the ceremony when the ten plagues are mentioned. It developed from this story that the ancient rabbis used to tell:

> When the Jews crossed over the Reed Sea into safety and the Egyptians were drowned, the angels wanted to sing. But God silenced them, saying, *What, human beings of my creation have drowned, and you want to sing?*

Each person at the table has a glass of wine. Children have grape juice. That night, wine is deliberately spilled. If there is no saucer under the glass, empty bowls are placed around the table within easy reach of everyone.

Everyone reads aloud together from the Haggadah. They say, *The Egyptians are children of God, as are we all, and we do not rejoice over their defeat.* Then all recite the ten plagues: blood, frogs, gnats, flies, cattle disease, boils, hail, locusts, darkness, and the slaying of the firstborn. As they do so, they tilt their glasses and spill drops of wine into the saucer or bowl before them, to lessen the source of their joy.

As the ten plagues are recited at the seder, everyone pours out a little wine or grape juice.

דֶם־צָרָה עֲבָכֶּים

עֵרוּב דִּכְבָלְשִׁין

בְּרֵך

אֲרְבָּה הַשֵׁךְ

כֶּל הֵבְכוֹרוֹח:

Matzah, Afikoman, and the Passover Tray. On the table is matzah for eating with the meal. There are also three separate pieces, covered with a cloth. Two and a half pieces are used for the bread blessings. The leader sets the remaining half piece aside for later. That piece is a symbol of the late-night meal, the last course, eaten in ancient times. It must be eaten last. This small piece is enough. All that is needed is one bite for everyone, as a taste. Setting it aside guarantees that it will not be eaten by mistake and that there will be matzah left for the purpose at the end of the meal. *Afikoman* is a Greek word that means "dessert," or "last food." And that is what the half piece is called. The afikoman is vital. The celebration cannot continue until everyone has had a bite of it.

European Jewish families started a game around this situation a few centuries ago. At a moment when the leader is not looking, or so the children think, they take the afikoman away and hide it. At the end of the meal, when the leader asks for it, the children produce it, but not before the leader promises to give them whatever present they have asked for.

The Seder or Haggadah. The table is set with candles, flowers, and china. Scattered about are dishes containing salt water for everyone to share in the dipping ceremonies. Beside each plate is a glass of wine and a printed Haggadah. There is also the extra empty glass for Elijah.

White is a symbol of purity, so the leader of a celebration may wear a white robe. He or she may sit on a

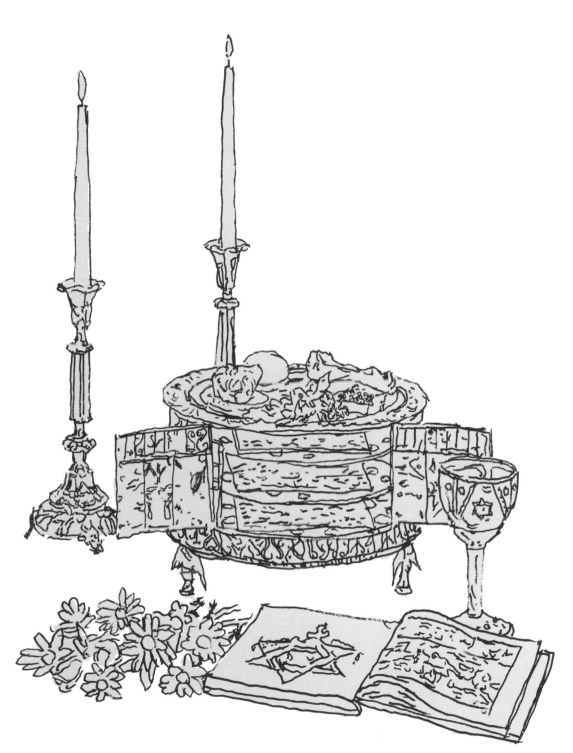

This matzah holder has a shelf for each of the three pieces as well as a place for the Passover tray on top.

pillow. The pillow stands for the divan of former times and is used tonight in the "leaning" ceremonies. In some homes, everyone sits on a pillow. On the table before the leader is a Passover tray with six symbolic foods:

Three *matzot*, covered with a cloth or in a holder.

Haroset, a fruit sauce made of mashed apples or dates, with nuts, cinnamon, and wine.

Maror, or bitter herbs. These may be lettuce or horseradish.

A Passover table

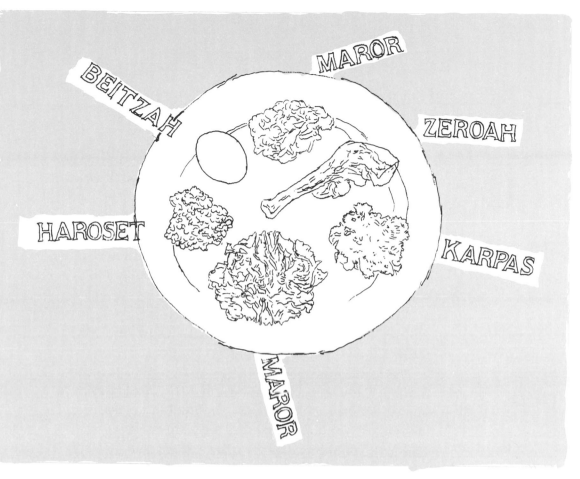

BEITZAH MAROR ZEROAH HAROSET KARPAS MAROR

A Passover tray with symbolic foods

> *Zeroah*, a symbol for the pesach lamb sacrificed in
> ancient times. This may be a roasted shank bone
> or a chicken wing or neck.
> *Karpas*, a symbol of the new spring crop. This may be
> celery, parsley, watercress, or any green vegetable.
> *Beitzah*, a roasted egg. This is a symbol of the hagigah,
> the ancient holiday sacrifice.

The Fourteen Steps. The leader conducts the celebration,
using the Haggadah as a guide. Everyone opens his

and her own Haggadah and follows along. Most Haggadahs consist of these fourteen steps:

1. Say the blessing over wine, praising God who created the vine, and recline (this is the first "leaning") to sip from the glass.

2. Wash hands. (A hand-washing ritual is performed in Orthodox homes. In Temple days hands were washed before approaching the altar. The ritual is a symbol of that act. The holiday table symbolizes the altar.)

3. Dip the karpas, the green vegetable (this is the first dipping), in salt water and offer praises to God for putting food on the earth to feed us.

4. The leader uncovers the three matzot, breaks one in half, sets one half aside, and in Ashkenazic homes, lets the children take it. Holding up the remaining two and a half pieces, the leader says:

This is the poor bread that our ancestors ate in Egypt. Let all who are hungry come and eat with us. Let all who are needy come to our Passover feast. Next year at this time may all the people of Israel be free. And may all humankind enjoy liberty, justice, and peace.

5. Children ask the four questions.

Everyone in turn reads from the Haggadah.

Tilt wine glasses for the Lessening of Our Joy ritual.

Sing "Dayenu."

The leader discusses the symbolic foods on the tray.

6. Wash hands again.

7. Bless the matzah and eat it.

8. Dip bitter herbs in haroset (second and last dipping) and eat it.

9. Make a Hillel sandwich of matzah and bitter herbs, and recline (second and last "leaning") to eat it.

10. Serve the banquet meal. ("At last!" the children call as the first course is brought out. The leader will see to it that everyone's glass has been filled with wine three times.)

11. In Ashkenazic homes only, the leader asks for the afikoman and agrees to the offer suggested by the children. The leader gives everyone a piece of the afikoman to taste and moves the celebration forward.

12. Say grace.

Fill everyone's glass with wine for a fourth time. Also fill Elijah's glass. The leader, or someone else, opens the door. Everyone rises to greet Elijah and sing "Eliahu ha-Navi" — Elijah the Prophet.

13. Offer praises to God.

14. Sing closing songs.

Baking matzah the old-fashioned way

The leader ends the ceremony by saying, *Next year in Jerusalem!* In Israel, where Jews are already near or in Jerusalem, they say instead, *Next year in rebuilt Jerusalem!*

The Second Day of Passover — Counting the Omer

Passover is the basis of another holiday, the Festival of Weeks, or *Hag Shavuot*. It does not fall on a specific date, as other holidays do. It takes place seven weeks from the second day of Passover. To find it, people must count. And on the second day of Passover, at the synagogue, people begin the count. They say, at the evening service, *This is the first day of the omer.*

An *omer*, in ancient times, was a bundle of barley. At Passover, the barley crop began to appear. To give thanks and to ask God's protection for the crop, people brought an omer of barley to the Temple on the second day of Passover. Then they began to count. This ritual disappeared when the Temple was destroyed. All that is left of it today is the counting.

And Counting the Omer, as the process is called, takes place every day for forty-nine days, and each week for seven weeks. Hag Shavuot, the Festival of Weeks, is celebrated the next day, on the fiftieth day. Pentecost, which means "fifty" in Greek, is another name for the holiday.

Shavuot celebrated two occasions. In ancient Israel it was an agricultural festival. At Shavuot, the fields were thick with crops swaying in the breezes. Wheat was ripe. So were the other main crops — grapes, pomegranates, figs, olives, and dates. To celebrate, people brought two loaves of bread baked from the wheat crop and baskets full of some or all of the first fruits to the Temple as gift offerings. Other names of the holiday are Festival of the Wheat Harvest, (*Hag ha-Katsir*) and Day of First Fruits (*Yom ha-Bikurim*).

Like their ancestors, the people of modern Israel also celebrate the holiday by dancing and singing in the fields. They decorate their homes with flowers and greens.

Shavuot is also a historical holiday. Linked to Passover by counting, it is the other end of the same historic event. Passover celebrates the freedom of the Israelites. Shavuot celebrates the event in the wilderness that gave meaning to the freedom. For, according to Jewish scholars, Moses received the Ten Commandments from God fifty days after the Israelites left Egypt. Jews refer to the Ten Commandments as "the Law." Another word for law is *Torah*. Shavuot is also called Time of the Giving of the Torah, *Zeman Mattan Toratenu*. At Shavuot, Orthodox Jewish men spend the whole night of the holiday at the synagogue, studying the Torah.

Children have their own ceremony. Around the time of Shavuot, the first graders who attend a Jewish day school are given their own first Bibles at a school celebration.

Passover
Around the World

Marranos

Marranos, the secret Jews of Spain, lived in great peril. Passover fell on the night of the full moon. That night, Spanish spies watched houses for signs of celebration. To avoid trouble, the secret Jews celebrated Passover two nights later.

There were secret Jews in Portugal and other places as well. Today there are still Marranos in Portugal, Mexico, Bolivia, and other lands. They no longer fear the wrath of the mob or the hostility of a government. But they retain the customs and habits their parents and grandparents handed down to them over the centuries.

The Marranos of Portugal today perform an extra ritual on the last day of Passover. They go to a river or stream and recite prayers and blessings before flowing waters. This custom actually belongs to another Jewish holiday, Rosh Hashanah. It is not surprising that customs change when they must be practiced in secret and in hiding. The children's game called Telephone provides an example of how such things can happen. One player whispers a message to a neighbor. The neighbor whispers it to the next person, and so on. By the time the message reaches the ear of the last player, it has changed.

Falashas

In modern times an unknown group of Jews was discovered by travelers to Ethiopia. For some 2,000 years, black Jews have been living there. Some say they are descendants of a union between the Queen of Sheba and King Solomon. Others say they are descended from the ancient Jewish tribe of Dan. All are devout Jews. Ethiopians call them Falashas, which means "strangers." They call themselves *Beta Israel*, Hebrew for "House of Israel." On Passover night, they gather in the yard of their synagogue to speak of the miracles that took place in Egypt so long ago. They pray for an Exodus of their own, some miracle to take them to Israel. For many of them, the miracle came to pass. In 1984, in a dramatic airlift, some 10,000 black Jews were flown to Israel and reunited with their people.

Mountain Jews

Jews living in the Caucasus, a mountain range in south Russia, wear "liberty clothes" on Passover eve. For men, this is a tunic with wide, loose sleeves. The

The Falashas, the black Jews of Ethiopia

women remove the veils they customarily wear over their faces and don their finest costumes and jewelry. They meet at the home of their leader, where they sit on the floor, on carpets, surrounded by many burning candles. The leader has before him a tray of matzah, haroset, and bitter herbs. He explains the significance of those foods and tells the Exodus story. When he reaches the point where the Israelites finally leave

Egypt, the men raise their hands toward Heaven and say, *May it be the will of God that the Messiah, the son of David, rescue all the people in exile, as the Lord our God rescued our ancestors in times of old.* The women answer, *Amen, may this be God's will.*

Samaritans

The Samaritans are an ancient Jewish sect who have been in Israel for over 2,000 years. They are the oldest Jewish sect in existence. Some of their beliefs differ from those held by most Jews. One example can be seen at Passover.

Most Jews believe that Moses received the Ten Commandments on Mount Sinai. The Samaritans say it was on Mount Gerizim. And on Mount Gerizim, the Samaritans celebrate Passover by reenacting the night of the Exodus as it is recorded in the Bible. Their celebration is living history, and people come from all over to watch the sight.

On the day of Passover eve, all Samaritans go to Mount Gerizim. On the slopes, they pitch the tents in which they will live throughout the holiday. They are few in number, under 300, and every member of every family will be there. The men all wear white robes.

Half an hour before sunset, the men stand reciting prayers. A priest gazes toward the west, watching the sun go down. He recites portions from the Book of Exodus. Boys dressed in white appear, carrying lambs. Two large cauldrons of water that boil nearby are for the lambs. So is the fire that burns in a deep pit. At the moment of sunset, the chief priest says the blessing.

He recites the words from the Bible: "And the whole assembly of Israel shall kill it in the evening."

At the signal the sheep are slaughtered. It is a time of rejoicing, and people kiss and embrace. Some fathers dip a finger in the blood of the lamb and daub it on the foreheads of their children, as a sign of protection. Meanwhile, men pour boiling water over the slaughtered sheep, which removes the wool. They examine the lambs to make sure they are perfect, then rub them with salt and lower them into the pit. As the lambs roast, the people eat unleavened cakes with herbs. The women and children then go to sleep or rest in their tents. The men watch the night and chant. At midnight, they wake everyone. Then, as their ancestors did some 3,000 years before, they eat the pesach lamb. They eat it with unleavened bread and bitter herbs. Their sashes are tied firmly around their waists, they wear sandals on their feet, and they hold staffs in their hands.

Sephardim

Hiding the afikoman is not a custom among Sephardim. They have a custom of their own for the matzah. Like Yemenite and Israeli Jews, they act out a "leaving-Egypt" scene. In one version, a child enters the dining room holding a piece of matzoh on his or her shoulder, and the following conversation takes place.

"Who are you?" someone asks.

"I am a Jew," the child answers.

"Where do you come from?"

"From Egypt."

"Where are you going?"

"To Jerusalem."

"What are you carrying?"

"I am carrying matzah, as my ancestors did the night they left Egypt."

In some homes it is the custom for everyone to rise and march around the table holding a piece of matzah on one shoulder. The march symbolizes a journey. If the scene is enacted in Israel, it represents the march out of Egypt. If the march takes place elsewhere, it represents a journey to Israel.

Among Baghdad Jews, the father asks the children questions. He might start with a question like, "Imagine that you were going to Egypt three thousand years ago. How would you prepare for the journey?" As is true of all Passover customs, the point is to keep the celebration interesting and the historic experience of the Exodus vibrant and alive.

Yemenites

Yemenites — Jews from Yemen, in southern Arabia — pile the Passover table high with lettuce leaves, radishes, parsley, horseradish, and other vegetables. They serve not one but many varieties of haroset, the fruit pudding. The haroset, as a symbol for clay, receives another symbolic ingredient. Yemenites add grains to the haroset, completing the symbolic brick. They may also sprinkle their clothes with incense, to make the night more festive. The Elijah Cup ceremony is not part of the Yemenite celebration. The custom began in Europe and never reached the distant land of Yemen.

Soviet Jews

The government of the U.S.S.R. is opposed to religion. Students are required to study scientific atheism in school. Soviet Jews who wish to practice their religion must do so in secret. Even the study of the Bible and the Hebrew language must be performed in secret. The government has made one concession on Passover: Jewish bakers may bake matzah. But Jews who wish to celebrate the holiday with a home ceremony must do so in secret.

The creation of the state of Israel has changed the attitude of most Soviet Jews. Israel provides them with a homeland, a refuge. They have a place to go if they should be expelled, or have reason to flee. Since 1948, when Israel was reborn, the Jews of Moscow, Leningrad, Kiev, Odessa, and other cities where there are large Jewish populations, have grown bolder. Despite government regulations, they go to the synagogue on Passover night in great numbers to show their solidarity. The synagogue is packed to overflowing. Those who cannot get in remain in the street.

Inside the synagogue, a rabbi, or leader, conducts a religious service. Outside, the multitude celebrates by singing Jewish and Hebrew songs. The government takes note of the celebration. The KGB, the Soviet Secret Police, watch from the rooftops and take pictures of the Jews. But the Jews find courage in their numbers and celebrate nevertheless. Thousands of them wish to emigrate to Israel, but they are not permitted to do so. Like the ancient pharaoh, the Soviet authorities will not let them go.

Jews arriving at the Great Synagogue in Moscow on Passover

Israeli Jews

In Israel, the whole country vibrates with activity as people rush to and from the marketplace preparing for the holiday. Flowers, fruits, and vegetables are on sale everywhere. The holiday begins with prayers at the synagogue. In Jerusalem, many people like to pray from a rooftop or hill so they can gaze upon the place where the ancient Temple used to stand. When they have said their prayers, they take their leave as they would of royalty, because God is the King of Kings. They walk slowly backward and bow to God in all directions. As they do so, they say, *May God Who makes peace in the high heavens grant us peace.* Then they go home to celebrate, and in a while the familiar and joyous sounds of the Passover celebration can be heard from open windows all over the land.

A new custom has been born in Israel that is likely to spread to Jews in other countries. The rabbis have decreed that an extra chair be placed at the table on Passover night. It is a symbolic seat for those who are not free to celebrate and those who wish to come to Israel but are prevented by their government from doing so.

Christians Learn About Passover

Relations today between Christians and Jews are different from what they were in the dark days of earlier centuries. Today, it is customary for Jewish families to invite Christian friends to a seder. Some Christians go further. Jesus was a Jew. Christianity grew out of the Jewish religion. And serious Christians are interested

The extra chair at an Israeli seder

in learning about the Jewish roots of their religion. To this end, some ministers and priests invite a rabbi to conduct a model seder at the church, to teach the Passover celebration. Passover has only one meaning: to celebrate the Exodus of the Jewish slaves from Egypt. A scholar priest or minister may teach his or her church members the fourteen steps that characterize this Jewish holiday.

Foods

For seven days you shall eat unleavened bread. (Exodus 12:15)

This biblical law gives a special character to the foods eaten on Passover. Not only is bread prohibited; cake, pie, pasta, and other leavened foods are also prohibited. Therefore, matzah, the dry, hard, square wafer (though sometimes it's round), is the main starchy food of Passover. It is not as flavorful as other breads. Perhaps that's why it was called *lechem oni*, poor bread, in the Bible. But what it lacks in flavor it makes up for in serviceability. Matzah does not go stale. Like any wafer, it remains edible for a long time and so is a perfect food to take on a journey.

To vary its use at the holiday, matzah is broken into pieces and fried with eggs. Some people crumble it into milk and add cinnamon. Matzah ground into a fine

A 17th-century woodcut showing matzah-baking

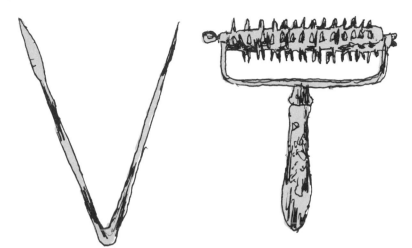

An 18th-century compass used to measure round matzah and a wheel to make perforations.

meal makes pancakes, matzah balls that are cooked in chicken soup, and other popular dishes.

The pastries of Passover are vanilla and chocolate macaroons (cookies made with ground almonds or ground coconut and ground walnuts) and yellow sponge cake.

Ashkenazim and Sephardim both obey the matzah rule. But each group has its own council of rabbis. And the council makes decisions for the group. Ashkenazic rabbis long ago prohibited the use on Passover of rice, corn, beans, peas, and peanuts. Sephardic rabbis made no such ban, and these foods provide many delicious dishes for Sephardic families at Passover.

The symbolic foods of Passover — those that are on the Passover tray during the celebration — are basically the same in all Jewish homes. Differences are small. For example, Ashkenazim use chopped apples as a base for haroset, the fruit sauce. Sephardim use dates instead. Moroccan Jews grind dates and nuts into balls. Iraqi Jews make a syrup of dates. Turkish Jews add raisins and orange peel to the mixture.

The banquet, the holiday meal itself, will be whatever a family enjoys on special occasions. The two councils of rabbis have created differences in what is eaten as a main course as well. The main course in an Ashkenazic home will be chicken, goose, or beef. Sephardim usually serve lamb, to commemorate the night of the Exodus. Ashkenazim take the view that lamb should not be eaten that night, in memory of the Temple that was destroyed in 70 C.E. and the lamb that used to be sacrificed there. But eating lamb has been a custom among Sephardic Jews for centuries. And in the Jewish tradition, a custom is as good as law.

Songs

There are many kinds of Passover songs. A Hebrew riddle song called "Ehad Mi Yodea? (Who Knows One?) is a history lesson as well. It is given here in English.

Who Knows One?

Who knows one? I know one! One is God Who rules in heaven and on earth.

Who knows two? I know two! Two tablets of the law, one is God Who rules in Heaven and on earth.

Who knows three? I know three! Three are the fathers,* two tablets of the Law, one is God Who rules in Heaven and on earth.

Who knows four? I know four! Four mothers of Israel,** three are the fathers, two tablets of the Law, one is God Who rules in Heaven and on earth.

Who knows five? I know five. Five Books of Moses,*** four mothers of Israel, three are the fathers, two tablets of the Law, one is God our father Who rules in Heaven and on earth.

*The three fathers are Abraham, Isaac, and Jacob.

**The four mothers are the three fathers' wives, Sarah, Rebecca, and Jacob's two wives, Rachel and Leah.

***The Five Books of Moses are the Bible.

A popular Ladino Passover song among Sephardic Jews is "Cuando Ejipto Fueron Salidos" (When They Left Egypt). The English words are as follows:

When They Left Egypt
When they left Egypt with their wives and children,
six hundred thousand sang;
the pharaoh pursued them under his red banner.
"Where did you take us, Moses, to die without
a proper burial, in the sands of the desert?"
"What can I do, my beloved people?
Pray to God and I will do the same."

Another popular Hebrew song is about an only kid, "Had Gadyah."

An Only Kid
Had gad-yah, Had gad-yah, my father bought for two zuzim.
Had gad-yah, Had gad-yah.

Then came a cat and chased the kid my father bought for two zuzim. *Had gad-yah, Had gad-yah*.

Then came a dog and bit the cat that chased the kid my father bought for two zuzim. *Had gad-yah, Had gad-yah*.

Then came a stick and hit the dog that bit the cat that chased the kid my father bought for two zuzim. *Had gad-yah, Had gad-yah*.

Then came the fire and burned the stick that hit the dog that bit the cat that chased the kid my father bought for two zuzim. *Had gad-yah, Had gad-yah*.

Then came the water and quenched the fire that burned the stick that hit the dog that bit the cat that chased the kid my father bought for two zuzim. *Had gad-yah, Had gad-yah*.

Then came an ox and drank the water that quenched the fire that burned the stick that hit the dog that bit the cat that chased the kid my father bought for two zuzim. *Had gad-yah, Had gad-yah.*

Then came the butcher and slaughtered the ox that drank the water that quenched the fire that burned

the stick that hit the dog that bit the cat that chased the kid my father bought for two zuzim. *Had gad-yah, Had gad-yah.*

Then came God, and God brought peace. *Had gad-yah, Had gad-yah.*

Here in English and Hebrew are the words of the song sung when the door is opened for Elijah.

Elijah the Prophet	*Eliahu ha-Navi*
Elijah the Prophet,	El-i-ya-hu ha-Na-vi,
Elijah, man of Tish,	El-i-ya-hu, ha-Tish-bi,
Elijah, Elijah,	El-i-ya-hu, El-i-ya-hu,
Elijah of Gilead,	El-i-ya-hu ha-Gil-a-di,
Speedily, and in our time,	Bim-hay-rah, b'ya-may-nu
He'll come to us,	Ya-vo e-lay-nu,
With Messiah, son of David,	I-ma-shi-akh ben-David,
With Messiah, son of David.	I-ma-shi-akh ben David.

A second song that is sung during the celebration is "Dayenu" (That Would Have Been Enough). The opening lines are:

> If God had only taken us out of Egypt,
> *that* would have been enough.
> If God had only given us the Sabbath,
> *that* would have been enough.
> If God had only given us the Torah,
> *that* would have been enough.

As Moses had commanded, Jews have been thanking God for their freedom by celebrating Passover each year from the night of the Exodus over 3,000 years ago to this day.

Glossary and Pronunciation Guide

Note: The sound *kh* is made by trying quietly, gently to clear the throat of an imaginary speck of paper.

Afikoman (afi-KO-men) A Greek word that means dessert. The piece of matzah that the children hide. On Passover night, the afikoman is eaten last. It stands for the lamb that was sacrificed in ancient times and that was the last food eaten at the celebration.

Ashkenazim (osh-ken-ah-ZEEM) Jews from central and eastern Europe.

B.C.E. Before the Common Era, which is the way Jews reckon time before Christ, or B.C.

Beitzah (bay-TZAH) Roasted egg, one of the symbolic foods on the Passover table. It stands for the hagigah sacrifice, the holiday offering of ancient times.

C.E. Common Era, or A.D.

Hag (KHAG) Festival, or holiday

Hag ha-Aviv (KHAG ha-a-VIV) Festival of Spring

Hag ha-Katsir (KHAG ha-ka-TSEER) Festival of the Wheat Harvest

Hag ha-Matzot (KHAG ha-ma-TSOTE) Festival of the Unleavened Bread

Hag ha-Pesach (KHAG ha-pes-AKH) Passover; Pesach; Festival of the Paschal Offering

Haggadah (ha-ga-DAH) The book or program for the Passover
ceremony. Also, the "telling" of the Exodus story and
the name of the banquet night in Sephardic homes.

Hagigah (kha-gi-GAH) Holiday sacrifice

Haroset (kha-row-SET) The fruit sauce on the Passover tray,
a symbol of mortar. The bitter herbs are dipped in it and
eaten.

Karpas (KAR-pas) The green vegetable on the Passover tray
that is dipped in salt water and eaten. It is a symbol of
the spring harvest.

Lechem oni (leh-KHEM aw-NI) Pauper's bread; bread of affliction; matzah.

Maror (mah-ROHR) The bitter herbs on the Passover tray,
a symbol of the bitterness of the lives of Jewish slaves
of ancient times.

Matzah (ma-TZAH) The unleavened bread the Israelites ate
in Egypt and on the night that they left.

Matzot (ma-TSOTE) Plural of matzah

Omer (O-mer) An ancient measure, a sheaf. Also, the ritual
of counting the days from Passover to Shavuot.

Pesach (pe-SAKH) Passover. Also, the paschal lamb that was
sacrificed in ancient times.

*A 19th-century matzah holder from
Germany*

Seder (seh-DEHR) Order. Order of the ceremony on Passover night. The Passover celebration in Ashkenazic homes.

Sephardim (s'far-DEEM) Jews from Spain, Portugal, North Africa, and the Middle East

Shavuot (sha-vu-OTE) The Festival of Weeks; Day of First Fruits and Season of the Giving of Our Torah; Pentecost.

Yom ha-Bikurim (yome ha-bi-ku-REEM) Day of First Fruits, Shavuot.

Zeman Herutenu (z'MAHN khay-ru-TAY-nu) Season of Our Freedom, another name for Passover.

Zeman Mattan Toratenu (z'MAHN ma-TAN tow-rah-TAY-nu) Season of the Giving of Our Torah, another name for Shavuot.

Zeroah (ze-ro-AH) The roasted shank bone or chicken wing on the Passover tray. It stands for the lamb that was sacrificed at Passover when the Temple stood in Jerusalem.

Other Books
About Passover

Adler, David A. *A Picture Book of Passover*. New York: Holiday House, 1982. The story of Passover for ages five to nine, with illustrations by Linda Heller.

Drucker, Malka. *Passover*. New York: Holiday House, 1981. A holiday book for ages eight to eleven, containing history, games, and recipes.

Goodman, Philip. *The Passover Anthology*. Philadelphia: The Jewish Publication Society of America, 1973. History, lore, poems, stories, and much information about the holiday for ages eleven up.

Greenfeld, Howard. *Passover*. New York: Holt, Rinehart & Winston, 1978. A short history for all ages, illustrated by Elaine Grove and designed by Bea Feitler.

Rosen, Anne; Rosen, Jonathan; and Rosen, Norma. *A Family Passover*. Philadelphia: Jewish Publication Society of America, 1980. Ten-year-old Anne tells about preparations for the holiday and its celebration, for ages six to nine. With photographs by Laurence Salzmann.

Index